Schirmer's Library of Musical Classics

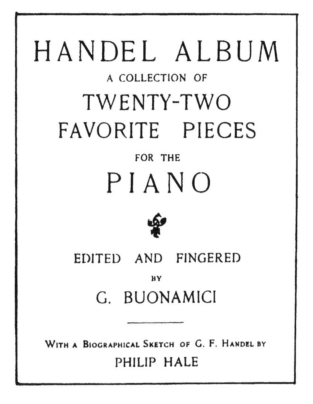

Vol. 43

HANDEL ALBUM

A COLLECTION OF

TWENTY-TWO
FAVORITE PIECES

FOR THE

PIANO

EDITED AND FINGERED

BY

G. BUONAMICI

WITH A BIOGRAPHICAL SKETCH OF G. F. HANDEL BY

PHILIP HALE

ISBN 978-0-7935-0583-8

G. SCHIRMER, Inc.

DISTRIBUTED BY

HAL•LEONARD®
CORPORATION
7777 W. BLUEMOUND RD. P.O. BOX 13819 MILWAUKEE, WI 53213

GEORGE FREDERICK (or Frideric) **HANDEL** was born at Halle, February 23rd, 1685. He died in London, April 14th, 1759. The son of a barber-surgeon, who did not wish his boy to be a musician, he studied music at first secretly, then, at the age of eleven, under Zachau, an organist in Halle. Although he played in public, composed, made a journey as a virtuoso, and was a settled organist, it was not until 1703 that he abandoned the law forever, and left his birthplace. Handel is to many the writer of oratorios. The absorbing passion of his life,. however, was the opera. He was both opera-manager and opera-composer. His first dramatic work was "Almira,"

(Hamburg, 1705). His last, and he wrote over 40, was "Deidamia" (London. 1740).

To tell the life of this busy man who, unlike Bach, his great contemporary, was in the world and of the world, would be to record his singular adventures in Hamburg, the journey to Italy, where he played in friendly rivalry with the younger Scarlatti and learned the beauty of Italian song, the breaking of the contract with the Elector of Hanover, the service to the Duke of Chandos, the famous competition with Buononcini, the struggles with spoiled, refractory singers, the pecuniary failures that crippled him for a time, though he died well-to-do, the varied fortunes of his cantatas and oratorios, the alternate adulation and indifference of patrons, the blindness that did not quench the light of his soul, the good ending, the burial in Westminster Abbey, and the apotheosis.

His figure was sturdy, even unwieldy ; his face was full of dignity, yet animated. Prone to anger and choleric outbursts, he was not ashamed to acknowledge a fault. A man of genuine devoutness, he, nevertheless, followed the custom of the time and swore profusely, sometimes ingeniously. Perhaps he had a love-affair in Italy ; but after he saw England. his heart does not appear to have been touched by woman. Kindly and charitable to a fault, he could not deny himself gigantic indulgence in the pleasures of the table. His courage was as conspicuous as his obstinacy. His works show the amazing fertility of his invention, yet he plundered nobly the works of other composers. He kept his promises and obligations—except in the memorable instance referred to above. His aims were noble, nor would he crook the knee to carry them out. He was unspoiled by praise or blame. All in all, a heroic figure in the gallery of musicians.

We have here to consider Handel as a pianist, and a composer for that instrument. Unfortunately, little has been handed down concerning his performance except vague words of enthusiastic commendation, as that Domenico Scarlatti, probably the greatest player of his age, always spoke of him with veneration, making the sign of the cross. Handel thought highly of Johann Krieger's "Anmuthige Klavierübungen" (1699), and, it is said, "in his youth formed himself a good deal on his plan." From Hawkins we learn that Handel practised incessantly, so that the keys of his Ruckers were finally spoon-shaped. His hand was so fat, at least during the

latter years in London, that the knuckles were concave, like those of a child. "However," says Burney, "his touch was so smooth, and the tone of the instrument so much cherished, that his fingers seemed to grow to the keys. They were so curved and compact when he played, that no motion, and scarcely the fingers themselves could be discovered." His hands were compared by Quin, the play-actor, to feet, and his fingers to toes. He accompanied with fine art. We know nothing about his fingering. when he played the piano, nor do we know whether, like Bach, he broke away from tradition and worked out a method of his own invention. We do know that whenever he appeared in public, as a pianist, in Hamburg, in Rome, or before Queen Anne, he excited lively admiration. The singer Faustina praised his "great style," and her husband "spoke respectfully" of him as a player of fugues. It seems from the testimony offered that though he was an admirable pianist, he was more remarkable as organist. At the piano, he was surpassed, undoubtedly, by Scarlatti, and possibly by Mattheson. As an organist. his only rival was Bach.

Handel's first collection of piano-pieces was published November 11, 1720. They were advertised as "Mr. Handel's Harpsichord Lessons," but the title reads "Suite de Pièces pour le Clavecin." In spite of Chrysander's denial, it is highly probable that they were composed for the Princess Anne, whose taste and judgment were as pure and fine as her hands were delicate and flexible. So, too. it is probable that the second and the third collections (1733.—) were written in part for pupils. The fourth collection appeared in 1735. The first set of suites is the one most highly esteemed, and Spitta claims that in them "Handel never furnished a more brilliant example of what he could accomplish in the line of piano-music."

These Suites, or Suites of Lessons, follow the custom of the time in excluding the pavans and the galliards, observing tonal uniformity, introducing at times the series of dance-tunes with a prelude, and closing as a rule with a gigue treated fugally. Handel's music for the piano is not so strictly claviermassig as that of Scarlatti, nor is it so daring in harmonic progressions, so epigrammatic, biting, witty in expression. On the other hand, you may search Scarlatti long for such sad, fragrant tenderness as breathes the sarabande from the E minor suite. Such an air suggests Chamfleury's comparison of the music of Boccherini to a flame-colored ribbon preserved tenderly in an olden rosewood bureau. The piano-fugues of Handel, whether intended for the organ or the piano, lack the romantic and the mystical feeling of Bach. They are matter-of-fact, full of English common sense. And in these piano-pieces Handel is alternately Italian or English. He is seldom. if ever, German in the sense of Bach. Some of this music is trivial, or as though written merely for the training of fingers. But there are pages of impressive strength and imperishable beauty.

PHILIP HALE.

Contents.

Appendix. (Arrangements.)

Fuga.

Allabreve.

1.

Sarabande.

Var. I.

Var. II.

Courante.

8

Air.

4.

Var. I.

Var. II.

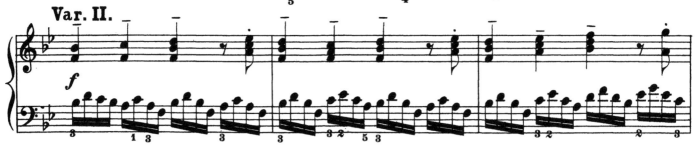

la 2da volta f

Var. III.

Var. IV.

Var. V.

Allegro.

la 2da volta un poco rit.

5.

a)

Gigue.

Allegretto vivace.

6.

Sarabande.

la 2da volta ritardando.

Gigue.

Capriccio.

Air.

Gigue.

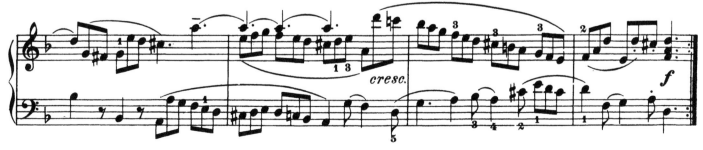

Prélude.

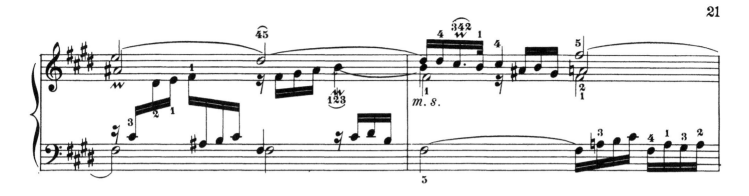

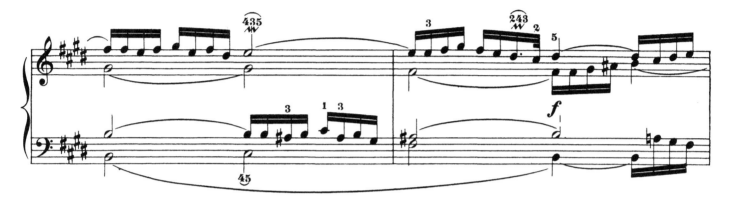

Allemande.

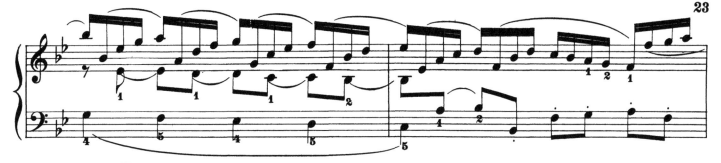

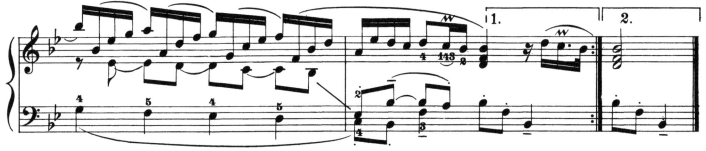

Passacaglia.

Moderato.

14.

tranquillo.

Animato.

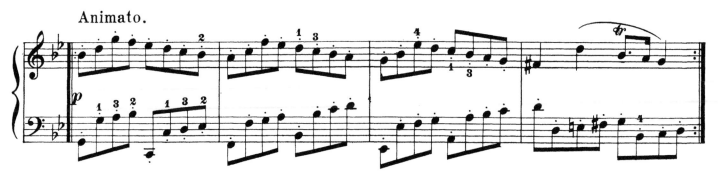

sempre più animato sino alla fine.

Allegro.

15. *bene accentuato.*

Gigue.

Fine.

Air.

The Harmonious Blacksmith.

Double I.

Double II.
Più mosso.

32

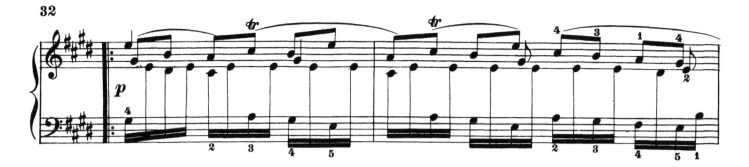

Double III.
Vivace.

Double IV.
L'istesso tempo.

a) opp:

Double V.
Sempre Vivace.

Gavotte.

18.

Double.
Tranquillo.

Allegro Vivace.

il Basso non legato.

Gigue.

38

March from "Saul."

Grave.

20.

See! the conquering hero comes.

From "Judas Maccabaeus."

Tempo di marcia, moderato.

Hallelujah! from "The Messiah"

G. F. HANDEL.

Allegretto moderato.